I Can

I Will

I Am

Finding Faith, Facing Fears,

Speaking Success

Andrea L. Battle

THIS BOOK IS DEDICATED TO:

Thank you Jesus for your love, peace, and for the opportunity to write this book. Stanley, my love, my rock, my best friend, I am so thankful to have you in my life. Mariah, Malia, and Mia, my little munchkins, thanks for the love, the laughs, and the hugs—you all are my world. Taylor, I am so proud of you; never stop achieving. I love you. Mother and Daddy, I love you guys so much; thanks for instilling so much into me. Ma, thanks for your continued love and support; I love you. Dominique, you've been a mother-figure, an encourager, a cheerleader, I couldn't have done life without you thus far. Jessica, blood could not have made us any closer; thanks for always listening and being a constant in my life. Ray, you keep me laughing; I love you big bro. Jasmen, your heart is so big and your love is so strong; thanks for always being there. Rashunda, my BFF, thank you for your strength, wit, and love. To my sister-cousins and sister-friends, Manchie, Shondy, Kym, Monica, Shamara, Angela,

Gabby (homescoop lol), Shari, Tracey, Whitney, Christie, Naketa (Hey Friend), Amenda (Dirl), Karen (thanks for your constructive criticism and support). Tami and Dr. Myles, thank you two for your mentorship, leadership, and support. Mom and Dad Winters for your prayers and putting up with teenager me and still loving me. Dad Gates for taking me to and from summer school and encouraging me; thank you! Uncle Stanley and Aunt Denise for always being a support system; I love ya'll. Aunt Sheila and Uncle Derrick for your love and encouragement. Lashonda, I love and appreciate you so much! Uncle Willie and James, love you guys. My boo-buddies, Chloe, Melissa, Catherine, thanks for always being an ear. Love to all of my God sisters and God brothers; Arie, Christina, Papa V., I love you guys. Mama V. I miss you so much; life has not been the same without you. To all of my friends, aunties, uncles, cousins, sisters-in-law, brothers-in-law, I love you all and appreciate your support.

TABLE OF CONTENTS

YOU. ARE. NOT

YOU. ARE. NOT… I am sure you have heard those three not-so-glorious words cross the lips of an enemy, a friend, or maybe even a parent. Perhaps someone told you, "You are not enough," "You are not pretty," "You are not smart," or "You are not deserving;" believe me when I say that I have heard all of these "you are nots" and many many more.

My most memorable experience was in high school when my school counselor, Ms. Wilbur, told me, "You are not college material." Of course, I may not have looked like it on paper—my grades were low, my behavioral record was trash, and I barely had the credits to classify as a 10th grader. But still, I was so deflated… who was she to tell me, Who. I. Am; in fact, who has the right to tell any of us who we are, what we can do, or even who we can be!

Sure, I allowed what should have been a few months of anger from my parent's divorce to last for several years, and yes, I failed the seventh grade. Plus, I served six months' probation for beating up a girl in my North Raleigh neighborhood—I was defending myself, by the way.

It's not that I regret defending myself, but I do regret the pure and utter hell I took my family through in that season. I cannot explain it, but somehow, Ms. Wilbur's words diminished the regret and self-loathing that I had experienced in my life up until that point and lit a fire in me that still burns to this day.

I CAN   I WILL   I AM

Words are powerful; from words, the world was created. With words, we commit our lives to one another. WORDS ARE POWERFUL. It is the words that we speak over ourselves and others that matter.

Have you ever taken a moment to recognize the negative words that have impacted you? Before getting too far into this book, I want you to take a moment to acknowledge the negative words that have defined you thus far. I am a firm believer in cleaning out space before bringing in new items. I want you to start this "cleaning" process by first acknowledging what people have said.

It is popular to say, "I don't care about what anyone else says about me!" However, many of us care! Not only do we care, but we have a reservoir hidden deep inside of us holding and protecting those words like treasure instead of releasing it like the garbage that those words are.

What have people said about you? Who has put negative words into the atmosphere concerning you? Maybe it was that boss or professor who berated you in front of your colleagues causing you to feel stupid and worthless. Or was it your "friend" or family member who is always putting you down to lift him or herself up? Perhaps your spouse refuses to stop deflating you with his or her constant demeaning words. Whatever voice you are listening to, I need you, for this process, to take a moment and acknowledge their negative words.

For some strange reason, we can hear a thousand positive words, but the negative ones are always the most lasting. Maybe the voice that you are thinking of actually has "receipts" to justify their words against you—as for me, I spoke so negatively about myself, it was easy for me to receive the negativity spewed at me by Ms. Wilbur and many others.

As you read this book, I want you to open yourself up to the possibility of a major change. A change in actions and a change in thinking. Today is the day for a new beginning. If you are anything like I used to be, you feel undeserving of another chance or a new beginning. You deserve a second chance; you deserve a new beginning. You just have to speak your new life into existence; I need you to believe it!

Even if your last infraction was an hour ago, you have the power to change the trajectory of your life, today. You can change your thoughts, and your actions at this moment. Don't stop believing in who God created you to be. Don't stop speaking positivity over your life. Putting yourself down all the time is not the way; it's okay to encourage yourself. As you read these words, this can be the first moment that you begin your journey.

Ms. Wilbur did not believe that I could start afresh when we met; I told her that I planned to go to college at the local university where my sister and her best friend had attended and that the person reflected in my records was not the person sitting before her. Not only did she not believe me, but she did not hesitate, she did not take one breath, she spoke over me like I was her creation and she was the creator. She spoke to me with authority, and without a gavel, she sentenced me—"You are not college material!" Her doubts and professional confidence attempted to kill my future.

Perhaps you may think that I am being dramatic when I say this, but at that moment, I saw her with the shovel, the bags, and the lime that she would use to cover up my scent. I was just another nobody; a kid with an attitude and a history of being nothing. I can only imagine the number of bodies she has sprawled around my high school. I can only hope that she stopped at some point—that she stopped killing futures.

I am sure that you've had a similar experience. If it wasn't someone else committing attempted murder, perhaps it was you who attempted to kill your future. You self-sabotaged because something in you could not handle that things were going well for you;

it wasn't intentional or maybe it was, but YOU got in the way of your goals. Thankfully, you still have time! You have time to change your life and to start afresh.

You can push through the war that you are in; you can push past the challenges that you're facing and wage war against whatever enemy is holding you back from reaching your dreams. You are deserving of a positive outcome. You have to believe these words; you have to believe it and say it; you must speak it to manifest it and produce it.

I want you to take a moment to visualize something or someone, even if the person is you, picture the doubt that is killing your future. I don't care if it's life-altering or trivial, picture something that you are trying to do, and whatever or whoever is between you and it. I want you to speak to it out loud and with confidence say, "I can, I will, I am."

Repeat it, "I can, I will, I am." That's what I did.

I looked at Ms. Wilbur square in her eyes, and I stated, "I can go to college, I will do what it takes to get into college, and I am college material!" I had no idea that success was right there, my success was waiting for me to speak it into existence. My words activated a change that I never knew I had access to. As I sit here, 19 years later, with a degree in psychology, a minor in Spanish, a Masters of Education, an Educational Specialist, and in the dissertation phase of a Doctor of Education, I wish that I could find Ms. Wilbur and tell her that she was WRONG!

But what's more important than finding Ms. Wilbur, is the satisfaction of igniting the fire in you that was ignited in me all those years ago. I am not trying to deceive you into believing that things became easy, instantly, but I want to teach you how to exercise your faith to make it in the face of doubt. I want you to ignore who you have a record of being. Maybe you have a record of being lazy, undisciplined, unfaithful, angry, or inconsistent. You can change that today.

There is an old saying, "Fake it till you make it." This age-old saying was created to encourage you to be optimistic through imitating confidence in whatever area you wanted to change. I am not saying that I don't agree with this saying, but that there is a better way—"Faith it till you make it." Being fake causes a false reality, but having faith causes hope. When I sat before Ms. Wilbur, I knew she would see right through me if I attempted to be fake, so I decided I would not be fake but I would show her the faith that I had in myself to succeed. All I needed was her to sign off on my classes that would get me on the college track; I am sure she thought I would come back to her with regrets, but the fire in me would not let me go back to her without a college acceptance letter.

I had no idea what I was doing at that moment in my life, but I knew that my faith was stronger than every single challenge that I had faced up to that point. My life was a complete disaster, but something in me felt at peace. God was setting the scene for a powerful outcome and all I had to do was go through the motions.

In case you are experiencing doubt, I want to remind you that you have the faith it takes to conquer whatever is holding you back. I will tell you about a process that I have used to succeed in the face of challenges beyond my wildest dreams. "I Can, I Will, I Am," is not some cheesy saying, but it is what I used to achieve goals that even I did not know that I could reach. My prayer for you is that by the end of this book, you find faith, face fears, and speak success. I cannot wait until you do!

I CAN

I have always made excuses for not reaching my full potential. I have blamed my parents for not creating me with a silver spoon in my mouth nor exposing me to all that the world has to offer. I have blamed those who doubted me, and others who I felt just wanted to see me fail. With all the blaming that I've done, the person who carries the most blame is ME.

I have been the biggest barrier to my success. It's hard to admit and maybe you can relate. But, even when things are going well, I find a way to self-sabotage, overthink, or make excuses for why I CAN'T do any given task. Of course, I am way better at this now. But, of all the people I have had to fight in my life both powerful and weak, my biggest contender has always been me.

I CAN...This phrase is so simple but holds so much weight. With only two syllables and four letters, it is a small giant. Saying it scared me because it has always meant something more. Saying, "I can" required me to commit; it required me to SHOW UP. It held this weight that I didn't want to carry. "I can" brought anxiety, doubts, fear, challenges; it tied me down. "I can" even embarrassed me; it embarrassed me every single time that I said that I could do something when in fact I could not.

I can remember times where declaring, "I can" humiliated me. In 6th-grade history class, I volunteered to read a passage aloud. "Can someone please read the next passage?" Ms. Preston asked. I had rehearsed the passage twice before volunteering and it was the 90s where children and teachers openly picked on you. I excitedly agreed, "I can read it, Ms. Preston!" I cannot remember what the passage was about, but I do remember when I read the word Arkansas loud and proudly pronounced Ar-Can-Saw, I said, "Are-Kansas" in the most confident manner. Of course, I had never read the word before; however, I can still hear the laughter that erupted in my classroom. My teacher chuckled too before Brooke yelled out, "It's Arkansas, you idiot!" Embarrassing right?

That day drove a wedge between me and, "I can." To think of it, I have allowed my negative "I can" experiences to sabotage me from reaching my goals. I am sure you can think of instances where saying it has embarrassed you—a time where you confidently declared you could do something and well, you actually couldn't.

I guess the real question is, should we see, "I can" as a bully or just embrace that we have underestimated it our whole lives? We shy away from it because we don't want to admit that committing ourselves to the hard tasks in our lives will take work, blood, sweat, and tears.

I had to get to know, "I can" and see it in a different light. It wasn't until that instance with Ms. Wilbur that I stumbled upon its power. My declaration that "I can go to college," reconciled me to, "I can." You see, after much thought, I realized that it is limitless; it is not confined by time, it is not confined by power, but it represents possibility. When you look at it as a possibility, then it starts to open the door of opportunity. You may not have the money right now, the status right now, or the network RIGHT NOW, but you have possibility and possibility can provide you the opportunity to find that one thing that you can do to get your foot in the door—that one thing is identified through the "I Can" mindset.

"I can" doesn't mean that it has to happen the first time or the second time. The "I can" declaration can come far before it becomes a reality. Saying, "I can" doesn't mean that we will be able to do it effortlessly; it may take work.

It did take work—a lot of work! There were years between my "I can" statement and my college acceptance letter. I want you to throw away your negative thoughts and accept that the first step to realizing your dreams is saying, "I CAN!"

It's easy to identify the roadblocks to your success and your dreams, but what have you done to identify the open road? It is vital that you look past ALL barriers, ALL challenges, ALL enemies, and see possibility. You will continue operating in the impossible as long as you continue to convince yourself that impossibilities exist. Anything is possible if a person believes (Mark 9:23). This world has conditioned us to reside in unbelief. In addition to unbelief, this world somehow forced us to accept that happiness and good things are reserved for an elite few—that wealth, beauty, status, joy, everything is unattainable. But this simply isn't true. Having the, "I can" mindset causes you to commit to a goal, to a dream, or a move. You are at a standstill because you are afraid.

When my oldest daughter, Mariah, was seven years old, she cried and complained that she did not know how to ride her bike. She was correct; she did not know how to ride her bike. However, she also had never tried. This may seem simple to you, but I had to tell her that she would continue to not know how to ride her bike as long as she refused to get on it. You see, you cannot do 100% of those things that you refuse to try! Once I dug a little deeper, I realized that her refusal to get on the bike stemmed from her fear of falling and hurting herself.

She is not alone in this, you have not gotten on the bike either. Not an actual bike, but you have not started something new; maybe you haven't started your business or gotten into a relationship because you have convinced yourself that you can't do it. Maybe you are not afraid of falling like she was, but you are afraid of failing.

She saw other kids in the neighborhood riding around our cul de sac and she wanted to ride too, but she couldn't bring herself to get on the bike. She could not commit to learning how to ride or identify an instance where she could get on the bike and not hurt herself. Until one day, she approached my husband like she was proposing a business deal; she asked him if he would promise her that he would not let her fall. She had convinced herself that as long as he would not let her fall, then she could ride her bike. He said that he would try but could not guarantee that he would stay by her side; he told her to promise him that if she fell that she would try again. Riding her bike went from an impossible feat to possible because she identified what she was capable of doing. Believe it or not, the first day she got on her bike, she learned how to ride.

You can start that business; you can get into a re-lationship, you can start something new, but first, you have to identify what, "I Can" looks like for your situation. No one wants to admit it, but the real issue that most of us have is that we want things to look like it does for those around us.

If our steps towards success don't look easy or do not look like the next man's success, then we give up. You mustn't give up, but you must identify your in-dividual "cans." Identifying the, "I can" in any situa-tion is possible once you face the fear that comes with, "I Cant." What are you afraid of? More than likely, the fear is blocking you from seeing what's possible in your situation.

For the next few chapters, we will look at what, "I can" looks like in the face of different situations. I be-lieve in you; you CAN do whatever you commit yourself to do!

I CAN: WORKING AROUND YOUR "CANNOTS"

When I was a special education teacher, I worked with a lot of students with various disabilities. Each one of their disabilities was laced with numerous, "I cannots." My little darlings had physical, intellectual, social, and emotional disabilities. Some struggled to learn because of brain injuries, processing weaknesses, there were so many reasons why some of my babies could not learn. I had some students who had no issues with learning at all, but lacked social skills and needed intense help with activities of daily living. I have served students in poverty, foster care, students who were abandoned, and mentally ill. Through these experiences, I realized that my students had legitimate excuses for their "I cannots;" however, I also saw these same individuals fight with everything in them to be able to say, "I can."

Saying "I can" does not mean that you don't have a legitimate case for why you cannot, but it simply means that you refuse to allow the "cannots"

to dictate your life. Refuse to settle for "I cannot" and change your vocabulary to "I can."

You CAN work around the things that you "cannot" do. When you operate with the mindset that, "I will do whatever I can to make it work," your "cannots" become unimportant.

One of my big sisters, Casey, got married a couple of years ago; her new husband, Josh, is a truck driver and she dreaded being away from him for weeks at a time. She never used the word, "depressed," but we all felt like she at least had the blues. She missed Josh and hated every minute that he was away. A financial guru, Casey has a Bachelor's degree in Finance, a Bachelor's Degree in Economics, a Minor in Spanish, and a Master's Degree in Accounting. At the time of her marriage, she had been working as a General Manager for a major hotel brand for many years.

One day, she disclosed to our family that she was unhappy with her career and unhappy with being away from her husband. She explored all of her options and found that she wanted to change her career.

Scene

Casey: I am quitting my job and will go to school to become a truck driver.

Pretty Much Everyone She Told: Wait, what? You cannot quit your job and become a truck driver; what about all of your degrees. What about your career? You cannot leave the corporate world. . .

Our Mother (behind her back): I did not send her to college to quit and become a truck driver; I was already upset about her working at a hotel. So she went from aspiring to be a Corporate Lawyer to a Truck Driver? I mean, she doesn't even drive particularly well.

End scene

Working around your "I cannots" will be difficult because everyone in your world will remind you of what you cannot do. I can remember the first day after my sister's last day of work. She looked at me and said, "What did I do?" She continued, "Can I really become a truck driver? I have not driven anything bigger than an SUV."

19

I must admit, it's not that I didn't believe in her, but I was pretty astonished by her change in career. I, too, questioned if she could do it. However, something in me, which I imagine was the same thing in her, was hopeful. She had faith; she saw possibility, all she had left to do was commit to the decision that she had made!

There have been very few occasions that I have seen my sister cry. During this process, I saw her cry on several occasions. Being the genius that she is, she had NO issues with the coursework; however, when it was time to put what she learned into practice, she struggled behind the wheel of the Semi-Trailer Truck. She could drive the truck, but could not perform any of the parking maneuvers.

Working around your "cannots" and converting them into "I cans" will take creativity, drive, and endurance. Casey and Josh had just enough money saved to pay all of their bills while she was in school—not a day longer. As the day of her driving test drew near, she put her fear away and took a moment to take inventory of the things that she could do well on the test.

She noticed that she was always being chosen by her teachers to show the class how to perform the Pre-Trip Inspections; she noticed that one of her peers, Derrick, was struggling with the inspections but did phenomenal with his parking maneuvers.

He could not do the pre-trip inspections and she couldn't park. She worked around her "cannots" by making a deal with Derrick. They made a deal that if she worked with him on the inspections, that he would work with her on parking. I would love to tell you that she grasped parking before her test, but this was not the case. She was able to complete a few maneuvers during her preparation for the test but was never able to perform the three hardest maneuvers necessary to pass the test.

On the day of the driving exam, Casey wore a shirt that said, "Faith;" not to sound cliché, but faith was the only thing that she could depend on because she could not park the semi-truck. The driving exam was a timed test; of course, she did well on the Pre-Trip Inspections, but she only had a specific amount of time left to prove to her examiner that she could park the truck.

Remember to be friendly to people when you are working around your "cannots." Casey wore a permanent smile on her face the entire time of her driving exam experience. She knew that she could not park the truck, but she was sure to make friends with the people who came between her and her license.

Casey was running out of time and was the last truck left in the yard. She had exhausted almost all of her time trying to park the truck, she needed a miracle. She had 15 minutes left before her time would expire. Like the scene of a movie, she looked at her examiner and saw that she was silently cheering for her, she looked across the yard at the main building and saw other examiners standing around watching. She felt a spiritual connection and them all rooting for her.

Every time she tells me the story, I get chills, but with 15 minutes remaining on the timer and enough time for one last maneuver, Casey pulled the truck up and she said she heard a voice clear as day say, "Pull up closer than ever before;" she pulled up closer and started the maneuvers and parked it into the dock.

CASEY PARKED THE TRUCK! SHE PASSED THE TEST. MY BIG SISTER IS A TRUCK DRIVER!!!

When facing your "cannots" make a plan, be strategic, and remember that your faith will take you across the finish line. Even if she did not pass the test the first time, Casey had to have faith and try. Numerous people did not get their license that day. But Casey was not one of them. She said, "I can be a truck driver" and she did just that! She is completing her second year as a truck driver—take that naysayers!

I CAN: EVEN THROUGH TRAUMAS

*Disclaimer: Protect your mind; if you are in a space where you are easily triggered by conversations of sexual or physical abuse, then skip this section entirely. The issues discussed in this next section are heavy; reader discretion is advised.

Every summer, my parents took my siblings and I to Georgia. My grandmother, Billie, would keep us with some of my other cousins in her ranch styled home. Stacey and her brother weren't visiting but actually lived with Grandma Billie because their mother, Lisa had died tragically in a car accident. We all were piled in her four-bedroom two bath home on a large plot of land.

A break from city living, Grandma Billie lived in the Deep South almost on the border of Florida. Summertime was the opportunity for my cousin Stacy and I to spend time together. A little under a year younger than me, we were inseparable. We did everything together, slept in the same bed, and played endlessly. Lurking in the background of summer

24

breezes and bike rides was a secret that she and I shared.

We were both being sexually abused; it all started at a very young age. It took a while for me to completely accept it, but my earliest memory of abuse was when I was probably barely four or five years old. It happened when one of my uncles, Uncle Chester, had Stacy and I on his lap. Holding her on one of his legs and me on the other, he molested us both. I can remember her being in this cute little dress and watching his hands violate her body and go back and forth to mine. Not completely understanding why this was happening, I can still, to this day, hear the sound of my mother in the other room. For many years I wondered, why couldn't she save us? Why didn't she know that something was going on in the other room?

While this is the earliest event of sexual abuse that I can remember, there were numerous other unwanted touches and violations by him and another uncle, Uncle Fester.

As a mother of three little girls, I cringe at the thought of what my and Stacy's young bodies and minds endured that day and many other days after that at the hands of Uncle Chester and Uncle Fester (of course I've changed their names—although I could care less about protecting their identities).

Uncle Fester did not start molesting us nearly as early, I am not sure if it's because he wasn't around but when he did start, he would sit at the foot of our bed for what seemed like an eternity before eventually climbing in and forcefully molesting us. I have always wondered if his conscience ever tried to take over as he sat at the foot of our bed or was he simply contemplating which one of us he would touch first— me or Stacy?

Sexual abuse was not the extent of what I experienced every summer. When I was not being sexually abused, I was enduring physical and emotional abuse at the hands of Grandma Billie.

Grandma Billie, I am sure, has nothing higher than an 8th grade education; she had endured countless abuses as a child herself—both physical and emotional. A mother of 11 children, she did the best she could having been traumatized herself. She was abused; so, she was abusive. Grandma Billie, Uncle

Chester, and Uncle Fester were not the only people to abuse me.

While my father was in the navy and my mother worked in Washington D.C., our neighbors in the apartment below us used to babysit me. I cannot remember the details because I was so young, but I have short snapshot memories of the hair pulling and the isolation. They would yank and pull my hair out when I did something wrong. As if that wasn't enough, they'd lock me in a room when they were mad; I can still hear the daytime television as I sit in the dark. I can't remember if I was in a closet or in a tiny bedroom, but there I sat alone and quiet. I was not allowed to speak.

Even to this day, I have a small aversion to the sound of daytime television. It's like I am transported to my childhood; the shows, the commercials, they all have a certain vibe. When I hear it, I remember. My mother did not realize what was happening to me; she just knew that my hair was falling out and she could not figure out why. The babysitters would tell her that they had to fix my hair because I was messing it up by playing in it.

I didn't tell my mother about the abuse until we moved to Virginia. She was furious; she returned to D.C. with her pistol hoping to find the abusers. They were no longer there. One was on the streets strung out on drugs, and my mother had no idea how to locate the other one. She still resents not being able to make them pay for what they did to me.

I can totally understand her feelings; why would someone pull a child's hair out as punishment or place a child in their formative years in isolation for hours? I'm sure that they did not realize or care about the potential damage that locking a child in the dark could have on their mental health and development. I feel fine now, but I am still unsure of how deeply that experience affected me.

Perspective is everything though, even in situations like this. When I finally spoke to my husband about it, he told me that even in the midst of the isolation and the loud television, God was keeping me.

He gave me an alternate perspective—perhaps they turned the television up and placed me in isolation so that I could not hear or see drug consumptions or drug deals that were happening. Who knows what the loud sounds of daytime television was masking. I am still thankful for his Godly perspective.

Abuse is wrong, no matter how you frame it. Once you grow up, everyone miraculously forgets about abuse — whether they are the abuser or witnessed the abuse, it is like none of it ever happened. For the person that was abused, a heavy weight remains. An unwanted residence is taken up in their brain — I try every day to evict the traumas that try to reside in my mind. The memories, the fear, the pain, all of it; I no longer have room for it.

As for the memories, I can remember waking up with my uncle's hand in my underwear, the pressure and pain, I remember fearing for my safety if I told. I remember feeling that Grandma Billie knew but did not care. I remember the feeling of the extension cord that she hurled against my young skin over and over again for small infractions. I remember the slaps across my face. I remember how each experience sent me deeper and deeper into this dark whole, I remember never doing anything about it.

When you have experienced abuse, feelings of hate and unforgiveness attempts to take residence in your soul, but you cannot let it! You CAN even through traumas. You can forgive, you can seek counseling and spiritual guidance. You can cry, you can scream, you can pray, you can forget, you can remember, YOU CAN...

You can do a lot of things, but you cannot ignore it; you cannot internalize it like I did. Perhaps if Ms. Wilbur would have dug a little deeper into my experience, she would have identified the source of my low grades and poor behaviors. She would have understood that I behaved badly because I felt bad about myself.

It's not my intention to cast a negative light on my mother, but she yelled at me when I finally told her about the abuses many years later. She asked me, "What am I supposed to do about it now?" I guess she felt helpless because Uncle Chester could not receive her wrath.

Uncle Chester had spent time in prison, and once he got out, he decided that he would turn his life around. Almost like an episode of Law and Order, he left home to get money for a bill and went missing. For almost a year, law enforcement searched for him.

Finally, a couple walking through the woods stumbled upon his remains. The autopsy revealed that he had been murdered—execution style.

My mother could not deliver her wrath to Uncle Fester either because he was in prison. Actually, he has been in prison my entire adult life. I have no idea how long his sentence is or what he is even in there for, but I doubt he sees the light of day any time soon.

Needless to say, my mother has never had the opportunity to "do something" about the abuses. As an adult, I have worked hard to mentally navigate my horrible childhood experiences. I don't know why, but as a child, I wanted someone to figure it all out without me saying a word.

As for Ms. Wilbur, it's not that I expected her to be psychic, but maybe she should have asked more questions and dug a little deeper so that she could have seen that my grades and behaviors were something that I could control.

I could not control the abuse, I could not control my parents' divorce, I could not control anything that had happened in my life, but I could control myself. I could control my bad grades and how angry it made my mother every time she saw them. I could make her feel something—it was like I wanted her to feel the pain that I felt. I not only controlled my grades, but I also had some control over my body.

I went through a smelly phase in 6th grade; yes, I was the smelly kid. Not only did I smell, but I also wore a bomber jacket no matter the weather and it sealed in the funk. Smelling bad pushed people away; I didn't want anyone near me, if no one was near me, then no one could ever put their hands in my panties again without my consent.

Of course, I was bullied about the funk and the fact that I wore the same jacket every single day. Maybe if someone had cared enough to explore why I wore that jacket so much and why I smelled, bad things could have changed for me a little earlier.

But that's neither here nor there—spilled milk. It is important, though, that we face the traumas that are crippling us. We must stop trying to mask our hurts all of the time. We cannot continue to ignore or hide what we went through.

I am not advising that you announce to the world that you were abused, that your parents divorced, or that you lost a family member, but I am advising you that you CAN deal with it in a healthy way. What that healthy way is, is for you to determine, that dealing with it is of the utmost importance.

It is equally important that you remain emotionally available to the youth around you; it is through connections that our youth receive direction. I would have done anything Ms. Wilbur had said, if she believed in me. She did not recognize the years and years of trauma that I had endured.

By the time I had met her, I had lost two uncles to murder—my father's brother was murdered in a drug house and like I have already mentioned, Uncle Chester was murdered. One of my mother's sisters was also murdered; she was found in her front yard with her face blown off. Her boyfriend did not want to tell his fiance that my aunt was pregnant with his baby so he did what any evil person will do, he killed her.

I had lost my uncle, my father's brother and Aunt Lisa (Stacy's mom) tragically to car accidents; the family still believes the man who was in the car with my Aunt Lisa wrecked the car killing her on purpose, but the cops never substantiated it. Two of my aunts died from cancer. One, my favorite Aunt Mary, died right around the time my parents' marriage started to fail, and of course, they eventually divorced.

My father was preparing to remarry when his father, my granddad passed away. Because he didn't want any drama with my mother, he did not tell me that he had died. In an effort to get in touch with him on the naval base, I called and one of the officers said, "Your father is in Michigan, didn't you know, your grandfather died." I can still hear my granny's voice on the line telling me that she was sorry that I wasn't told and how much she wishes I was in Michigan. I honestly never thought my dad and my relationship would ever repair after that—it has, but it's been a long road.

I had adored my grandpa; I didn't deserve to find out about his death that way. I can still remember his smile, the taste of his homemade ice cream and lemon pound cake.

I could honestly go on and on about the traumatic losses that I have endured, but I think you get the picture. When I say you can even through traumas; I am saying this as someone who has—through traumas.

I am not trying to put pressure on you to get over the things that you have gone through, but what I encourage you to do is acknowledge them. Find a safe place and mental space to deal with the things that have happened to you. Seek out professional help because it's necessary and refuse to let your hardships take control.

Take the time to identify what you can work through. It took many years for me to acknowledge the sexual abuses in a healthy way; I was 19 years old and in college, before I allowed myself to completely remember my Uncle Chester molesting my cousin and I. I can remember having the memory vividly and immediately reaching out to my university's counseling center to cope. Don't ever be afraid to seek help, join a support group. Do something! And don't get discouraged if your first cycle through therapy sessions, groups, or whatever don't "cure" you; the intensity that caused the trauma will be the intensity necessary to soothe it. Don't be afraid to ask for help or to do whatever it takes to fix the issue.

You can! Snatch the power back from that issue that is attempting to steal your joy, your hope, your purpose. Do something! I believe the world produced the saying "Live, Laugh, Love" as a way to encourage you to do something; but if can interject one thing: Don't just, "Live, Laugh, Love," but also rest, relax, cry, talk, pray, share, fight, build, hug, release, focus, connect. You can by any healthy means necessary!

I worked at a residential treatment facility my senior year in college. I was majoring in psychology and my boyfriend (who is now my husband) referred me to get some much-needed experience with mental health. When I first started working there, I worked as a Child Care Worker (CCW) on a girls unit of 20 girls in crisis. These girls either came from jail, a mental hospital, or were court-ordered to live in the facility because of their extreme mental health challenges. As a CCW, I had to conduct small groups with the young ladies, nothing intense, but we had some very moving conversations. One of those conversations stuck with me, even to this day.

I was conducting a group with about 6-8 girls one day. We were discussing bad habits; the conversation was very light-hearted. We laughed and talked about the bad habits that we had and the bad habits of our loved ones. I shared with them that I used to bite my nails, several talked about how they still bit theirs, others discussed twisting a piece of hair, most of them talked about how they could not stop cursing. We laughed uncontrollably and harmoniously sang, "Ewww" when one of the ladies discussed picking the lint from between her toes. Finally, I got to the last girl; I was silently celebrating how we got through an entire group without the girls verbally or physically fighting, when she totally blindsided me.

She wasn't verbally or physically aggressive, but she somehow converted our light-hearted session into something different. When it was her turn to speak, she said something that has challenged my thinking for a long time. She rolled back her sleeves and uncovered an innumerable number of cuts on both of her arms. A few were fresh and others were scars. The cuts went from her wrist all the way to where she had bunched the sleeves of her long-sleeve shirt. I can remember her staring at her tattered arms.

She stared at them for what seemed like an eternity when she looked up and said, "I am a cutter; my bad habit is cutting." Without giving any space for a response, she went on. "I started cutting myself two years ago when my mom passed away, and I have cut myself ever since to deal with my problems. Cutting is my coping skill." I held my breath as she continued, "I was meeting with my therapist yesterday and she asked me if I can remember what any of my cuts were for—like she wanted me to point at them specifically and tell her what they were for." We were all stunned; no one breathed, no one spoke. She looked around and said, "I could not tell her; even the newer ones, I could not tell her what they were for."

It was like she was having an epiphany before my eyes. She said, "I cut to cope, but here I am with a scar that has absolutely no meaning. It's like I understand now why I need to stop cutting myself." Her self-reflection was mind-blowing.

Can you identify with this young lady? How are you manifesting your traumas? Believe it or not, you are doing SOMETHING to cope. Perhaps you have enlisted the help of a therapist or have joined a support group OR perhaps you have done nothing at all. Maybe you are coping through your use of alcohol, drugs, opiates, promiscuity, or self-harm. Only you know what you are doing to "handle" your traumas. We either do nothing or something unhealthy to heal our internal scars.

Saying "I can even through traumas" is saying that you are willing to agree to do something, *POSITIVE*, to handle your scars. If you have not already, I want you to take a moment and list the things that you can do to cope with life's challenges. If you already have a "coping skill," I want you to assess the skill to see if it is actually helping you to cope. The young lady referenced above cut herself to cope, but she did not actually "cope." Her cuts did not "heal" the internal wounds left by her mother's death. She said herself that none of the scars had meaning.

Neither my bad grades, bad behaviors, nor poor hygiene could help me cope with my parents' divorce, the deaths in my family, nor did they help me to cope with the fact that two of my uncles molested me. Instead, my poor coping skills caused me to fail the 7th grade, they made me self-sabotage, and ultimately placed me before a school counselor who didn't care about me or my future.

I want you to rid yourself of the thoughts that are telling you that you cannot handle the hand that life has dealt you; instead, I want you to look at your hand and make the decision to play, your best, anyway. It does not matter if you win the game, play your hand the best way you know how!

I want to leave you with one last thought. You've more than likely had traumatic experiences. Even with the trauma, you have a choice to make; you can be happy, be successful, have fun, write a book, start a business, fall in love, have peace, play a sport, learn an instrument, mentor someone else, teach a class, start a group, you can do something. Please do something because...

YOU CAN--even through traumas!

I CAN: IN 24 HOURS

Have you ever thought about the fact that everyone—everyday folks, military personnel, missionaries, superstars, homeless individuals, famous athletes, billionaires, etc., have the same 24-hour day? I am not trying to make you feel bad about the way you spend your day, but when you think about the things that people do with their time, it is mind-blowing. Just think, Michelle and Barack Obama, Steve Jobs, Martin Luther King Jr., Nelson Mandela, and Issa Rae; they all made an impact with the same 86,400 seconds that we have. They all used the time that they had—every moment to make a change. They changed entire nations, they created a future, they were pioneers in their individual roles, these people changed the world—our world.

I have heard people ask, what would you do if you were only given 24 hours to live? But, I want to ask that in a different manner. What are you doing each 24 hours, that you are given, to truly live? What are you doing to give each day purpose? From this point forward, I want you to give each day meaning. It is so easy to become complacent about life's challenges. Do you truly want to meet your goals?

Imagine your goal is at the top of a mountain. What are you going to do to reach the top? Will the rocks and height of the mountain discourage you? Or will you find a way to have faith, face your fears, and speak your victory?

We all have a choice how we spend our time and the time we will invest in reaching our dreams. You can make the best out of those 86,400 seconds, but you have to work hard to do it. You will have to devise a plan, you may have to get up early, and go to bed late some days. You may have to stay in constant prayer, you may have to fast, you may have to go back to school. You may have to hustle. But, you can. You can make the best of every 24 hours that you are gifted.

First, you must be willing to sacrifice. What are you willing to sacrifice to be successful or to find your purpose? Is it a person, is it a thing, is it a job, or is it a mindset? You will have to sacrifice negative thinking and/or negative speaking; you may even need to offer up that friend who refuses to change and is holding your purpose captive.

You may have to start over. Have you ever considered starting over? Perhaps you can't reach your promised land because you are afraid of starting over. The fear of starting from scratch is debilitating; all you can see is the time that you have put into your current situation, but you are failing to see the potential in a reset.

You. can. reset.

Starting over is not a negative construct; change your focus. Focus on the positive aspects of starting over! As a military brat, I had numerous opportunities to start over. By the time I had met Ms. Wilbur, I had already attended 10 different schools. I would start the school year as one person and realized that that did not go over well and I would totally reinvent myself. I remember when I attended one school in Virginia, I spent the few months I was there with a fake New York accent. I thought it was cool and so did my peers, so I kept doing it. I kept speaking like a New Yorker. It is laughable when I think about it now, but that is how I started over! I would change my style, my friend group, I reset until I found the me that I was comfortable with.

I am not telling you to lie and be fake, but what I am saying is in order for you to find where you need to be, you may have to try something new. You may have to do something similar to what I am doing—I am changing careers. I am learning to accept the fact that 2 of the 3 degrees that I have, my leadership certification, and current doctoral degree is in a field that I am not even sure that I want to remain in.

It is scary to think that I may have wasted time— that I sacrificed years and resources for something that I may not ever do again. However, it is even scarier to think that I will spend every 24 hours until retirement doing something that I dislike. I cannot allow fear and worry to dictate my 24 hours.

Please note: Your acceptance of a restart doesn't erase all of the work that you've done previously. In fact, everything that you've done up to now is meaningful and powerful to helping you through this restart and those skills that you attained will be crucial in your new moves.

Perception is crucial when saying, "I can!" 24 hours may not seem like enough time, and you may be clueless where to begin, but you cannot allow what you see around you to deter you from reaching your goal. Make sure you have a vision for your time; don't just walk blindly. Seek God for your purpose and His plan for your life. Be sure to use your 24 hours in a meaningful way!

As you reach mastery with "I can," don't forget to remain balanced; I define balance as a mix of 'Yes I can' and 'No I won't.' I know that may seem comical and/or cutthroat, but in order for you to properly use your 24 hours, you are going to have to learn when to agree to give of your time and when to set boundaries. You shouldn't say no all of the time, but you also cannot always say yes. You are not using your 24 hours wisely if you are constantly giving it up to others. What are you leaving for yourself? When are you rebuilding, when are you meditating, praying, and renewing your mind? You are no good to yourself and certainly no good to others if you do not create a balance in your life.

You may have the skillset, you may have the time, and you may have the resources, but that does not mean that you are obligated to move on every situation. I used to get caught in that trap; I used to give nine hours to work, two hours traveling to and from work, daily. I would give four hours to cooking, cleaning, doing laundry, daily. 4-5 hours coaching and ministering to friends and family weekly, 5-6 hours to church weekly not to mention the 45-minute commute. You get the picture; I never set time away for myself. I literally gave away every minute of my life. Saying, "I can in 24 hours" is saying that I can achieve balance. I can set boundaries and consistently enforce them. The world will not end if you say, "No, I won't" and mean it.

I have to use self-talk sometimes to coach myself into saying, "No, I won't." Some people are skilled at saying it, but I have never had that skill. Maybe you are like me and you desire to please people. You cannot allow your people-pleasing mentality to hinder you from being balanced. Attaining balance is not an all or nothing mindset; a balanced mindset is the perfect mix of, "Yes, I can help you with that task" and "No, I won't be able to help you with that task." It's not just making those declarations, but real balance is having peace with your decision.

You can move mountains in those 24 hours; you just have to get your timing right. Saying, "I can" in general, isn't easy, but you can condition yourself. It will make a world of difference in your life!

I WILL

Did you know that you can "will" things into existence? I am not talking Sci-Fi or television stuff. I am talking real life; you can believe in something so hard that it happens. You are able to manifest through your faith. In order to "will" something into existence, you must have faith.

Let me give you an example: I hate losing; I mean I absolutely, positively HATE losing. I will do whatever it takes to win at any and everything that I am doing. I don't like losing simple things like rock-paper-scissors. I spent the first three months of the COVID-19 pandemic sitting on my rear-end with absolutely no drive to exercise. However, my mother-in-law convinced me to get a Fitbit and I instantly became a workout beast. I literally went from almost no exercise to being number one on my family's 5-Day Workweek Hustle challenge; I completed 71,375 steps my first week. I walked, I ran, I danced, I jumped; I did whatever I could to get steps. I'd do anything for steps; I'd wake up early in the morning to go to the restroom and do a 20-minute workout before going back to bed and sleeping it off. I walked in place, I snuck out the house and walked my neighborhood. I did whatever I could to win.

Willing something into existence also involves work, but it is work that is directed at what you are willing. For instance, I did not say, "I will win the 5-day workweek challenge" and continued to sit around. I had to change my habits; I had to change my focus and my behaviors. Have you ever considered how important change is in reaching your goals? Saying, "I will" activates faith! The next thing you have to do is commit to the "works" needed to "will" it into existence.

James 2:26 (New Living Translation) states, "Just as the body is dead without breath, so also is faith dead without good works."

Every fiber of my being wanted to win the "5-day workweek hustle." Well, let's just say that my mind wanted to win, but my body had become accustomed to comfy sofas, afternoon naps, delicious snacks, and binge-watching television shows. To say that my body did not agree with my desire is an understatement. My back, my shoulders, my shins, my calves, my ankles, pretty much my entire body hurt. My body had enjoyed the sedentary quarantine lifestyle; I had to change my habits to "will" my win into fruition. I had to be willing to change.

I want you to look at, "I will" as what you will specifically do to make something happen in your life. In order to, "Faith it till you make it" it is vital that you identify specific moves or things that you will do to accomplish your goal.

I have a close friend, Sage, who started a non-profit over a year ago; during the Christmas season, she put together her first successful program. She provided the children of over 50 families with new shoes, clothes, and gifts. However, soon after, she felt stagnated because of her 9-5 job, husband, child, and new home. Sage had a hunger to do more with her non-profit but could not find the time to be a good professional, wife, and mother while moving forward with her vision. It was already June and she complained of having little time to do anything for her non-profit. I encouraged her to have the faith that she had when she created the organization. We sat and reviewed her goal, then I helped her identify her "I cans," and "I wills."

Sage was going on and on about all of the things hindering her from doing more with her organization. I encouraged her to make one goal. I helped her to realize the need to figure out her "I can" and her "I will." We jotted it down:

Goal: Start a fundraiser.	
I can research fundraisers and identify the right fundraiser for my organization. **I can** write a fundraising plan. **I can** identify a team of people to serve on my fundraising team. **I can** raise $500	Over the next week, **I will** identify 5 fundraising ideas. **I will** use the ____ program to create a fundraising plan. **I will** have my mother, sister, best friend, dad, and cousin on my fundraising team. **I will** invest $150 to start the fundraising process.

Most people are inundated with time constraints, family demands, or various challenges. That is the value of "I will." Saying "I will" forces you to be specific in planning what you will do based on the realistic "I can" statements that you had previously made!

People always ask me how I have managed to have two graduate degrees, three children, and a husband, my answer is the same. God blessed me; He blessed me with a will to succeed and I have learned not to look at obstacles but at options.

The last month of my twin pregnancy was difficult to say the least. My stomach was massive and I experienced extreme pelvic pain and ligament stretching. My stomach was so heavy that the Dr and I feared it would collapse. My doctor prescribed a back band to hold my stomach up. Because of my first daughter's premature birth and the presence of massive fibroid tumors, my pregnancy was high risk. I had to schedule my sweet twin daughters' birth while at the same time working to finish my Educational Specialist Degree.

Casey called me crazy when I, only days after having my babies, was breastfeeding and working on a project at the same time. I had them on Tuesday and my project was due on Sunday at 11:59 pm. With the help of my husband and mother, I was recovering from a cesarean section, breastfeeding two infants, caring for a three-year-old, and doing graduate work. I have to say, 30-year-old me definitely had the will to do things that I'm not sure if 34-year-old me even have the desire to do. But I must admit that I was hungry for success. I knew that I wanted a leadership position and that it would take a higher degree to set me apart in my school district.

My goal was to complete my class with a "B" or higher; crying babies and swollen lactating breasts were no match for my will. I made a specific plan that entailed my mother staying with me for the first six weeks of my twins' life and a specific process that allowed me to continue with my graduate coursework. Saying, "I will" is saying that nothing will stop me from making things happen because I have a plan.

Don't be afraid to speak your will out loud. I can remember saying, "I WILL NOT LOSE" the 5-Day Workweek Hustle; because of that declaration, I had the most steps and I was the winner. The same is the case for getting into college. I did not just tell Ms. Wilbur, "I will go to college" and then continued to make bad grades and displayed bad behaviors. I worked endlessly to get into college. I had to retake all the classes that I failed or made low grades in; because of this, I did not have many electives. Could you imagine going through high school and taking almost no electives? It was one of the hardest academic trials of my life, this coming from someone with graduate degrees. It was hard, but my "will" to get into college made me try harder.

When you say, "I will," you are preparing the atmosphere to do whatever it is that you tell it. The Bible speaks of moving mountains with a mustard seed of faith; the verse ends by saying, "Nothing will be impossible if you believe" (Matthew 17:20). You WILL move mountains if you believe. Do you believe in yourself, though? Like, believe that you are capable of moving figurative or literal mountains.

There are times that I believe in myself or something at such a level that I believe that I can make it move, supernaturally. Of course, I have never moved a literal mountain; however, I have seen major issues best known as "mountains" moved in my life. Truth is, it is rare that I am moved by my mountains because I "will" my mountains to move. When you have a will to do something you are saying that you have an immense determination to do it.

What is it that you have an immense determination to do? Name it right now, say one thing that you are determined to do. What has stopped you? Have you grasped it yet; that success is at the tip of your tongue? What words are distracting your will or your motivation to move? Do you have a Ms. Wilbur telling you that you cannot move forward? Or, is it you? Are you stopping you?

I WILL: STOP PROCRASTINATING

Are you a procrastinator? Okay, maybe you don't identify as one, but do you have a bad habit of putting things off until tomorrow, or the next day, or even the next? Does your "I'll do it tomorrow" turn into it never happening at all? You just might be a procrastinator. Procrastination is a huge barrier between you and your goals or dreams. Believe it or not, putting your dreams off can actually kill your dreams. I'm sure you remember Langston Hughes' poem, "Harlem" from high school literature class; he spoke poetically about what happens to a "dream deferred." I pray that I have caught you before you've allowed your dreams or goals to "dry up like a raisin in the sun or fester like a sore and then run." Because dreams are not meant to be put off; your goals deserve a chance to be realized.

While we are not all inherently passionate people, we all have things that we are passionate about. However, for some of us, passion is short-lived because we succumb to procrastination. Overall, I am not a procrastinator; however, I can display procrastinator tendencies. I think it's safe to say that there are things that we all "put off" until tomorrow. But oftentimes, tomorrow never comes. We put off business ideas, going back to school, learning a new skill, starting non-profits, making connections, networking, branding, creating, we allow our dreams to dry up like Langston Hughes eloquently states. We miss our seasons, we miss opportunities, we allow others to live out our possibilities and then we wallow in envy.

We listen to our elders speak of regrets and "should've, could've, would'ves" but we fail to see ourselves in them. We fail to see that every day that we refuse to realize our dreams, we are accepting a fate filled with regret. God has given us dream after dream, idea after idea, but we don't move on any of them. What is it in us that is afraid to succeed? We all want success, flashy cars, big houses, financial stability, but most of us only put forth mediocrity. Then, we have the nerve to scowl at those who make it and compare ourselves saying, "I could have easily done that!"

You are right! You could have easily been the next social media personality, top lawyer, teacher of the year, trucking company owner, successful non-profit, etc. I want you to transition from going on and on about what you "could have done" into making plans and speaking with authority about what you will do. Say it with me, "I will stop procrastinating."

For some of you, your next big idea, your next move, and your future depends on you saying, "I will stop procrastinating." Take a moment and look at the few types of procrastinators that I have identified below. This list isn't exhaustive, but I am sure that you can relate to one or more of these:

First, there is the...

- "I can do it tomorrow" procrastinator:

- o This type of procrastinator confidently exclaims, "I can do it tomorrow." It does not matter what the "it" is, it will be done "tomorrow." "Tomorrow" does not necessarily represent the next day. By saying, "tomorrow," the procrastinator is articulating that the task is not important enough to complete right now, but it will be done at some point in the future.

Next, we have the...

- "I work best at the last minute" procrastinator:

○ This type of procrastinator loves to boast that he or she works best under pressure. This person enjoys sharing examples of how they became the victor in the very last minute. You will hear them say things like, I turned that paper in at 11:59 and it was due at 12:00. Then they go on and say that they made a high "C" or low "B" on something that they did not start until the last minute. Ultimately, this person wants you to celebrate their refusal to reach their full potential masked as a win. They never share the times that this method has backfired.

Then we have the...

- "Fashionably late" procrastinator:

○ This type of procrastinator does not complete anything on time, and then when they do finally complete a task, they want you to accept what they completed even though it is tardy and no longer needed. They say things like, "at least I still did it; I could have just given up!"

Lastly, there is the...

- "Always busy" procrastinator:

o This person is ALWAYS BUSY. However, when you dig a little deeper, you find that what they had to do wasn't important at all. These individuals use day to day responsibilities as excuses not to realize their potential. They exacerbate small tasks and love to say, "Where do you find the time to do anything else?"

Procrastination breeds excuses and failure. Can you see yourself in any of those examples? I have procrastinated about losing weight and used the "always busy" excuse to justify my unwillingness to do something about the extra weight. Let's agree that we will make the necessary moves to meet our goals and realize our dreams. The "I will" principle can help you. Like I have mentioned before, it is vital that you commit and be specific about what you "will do." You are not only to be specific, but it is also important that you place a timeline on your "wills."

I will register my business as an LLC. By next Friday, I will have the paperwork completed.

Procrastination and planning cannot occupy the same space.

Some of you are still not convinced; I know which ones you are. You are the, "I work best at the last minute" procrastinators. Because you have seen success with your practices, you don't see the need to change.

What if I told you that those of you last minute-workers are so powerful that you are probably capable of creating the next million-dollar idea, but you are limiting yourself by waiting till the last minute. You are hindering your brain from stretching to a bigger dimension of thought. Frankly, you are being lazy and irresponsible when you limit yourself to "last minute" practices.

As procrastinators, we become self-sabotagers. We sabotage our potential and water down our abilities. I haven't researched this, but I'm pretty sure you procrastinate because you are afraid. You fear putting your all into any given goal or dream and failing, procrastination makes you feel better at failing. This way of thinking is flawed because in actuality if you put your all into something and fail, you are getting closer to finding a solution.

Do you realize that it takes failure to create success? How else would pharmaceutical companies know what drug works for what ailment if trials aren't done.

Do you hear what I am saying? Without "trials" you cannot reach your goal or dream. It is through trials that we find solutions. I want you to stop using procrastination as a reflex to your fears and instead give your all and plan your next move. You will figure out the solution to the problem that is keeping your goals and dreams from being realized. You will not allow your dreams to die because you keep putting them off. You will reach for your goals today, you will create, you will get back up when you fall, you will discontinue your last-minute practices, you will create a timeline, you will stop procrastinating! Say it again, "I will stop procrastinating."

I WILL: OVERCOMING MY FEARS

Over the years when I've shared my story with others regarding my drive to be "College Material," I have had individuals stop me and share stories of people who doubted them or family members and friends who did not believe in them. However, one consistent theme that I have seen in people that I have talked to is "Fear." For those who are afraid to enroll in college, they are all held back by the fear of one or two classes. Don't get me wrong, I used to be terrible at math; however, I could not let College Algebra stop me from going to college. This may seem foreign to some of you, but I know that this is hitting home for some of you. You are afraid to take the next step because there is something included in that next step that you are afraid of.

I know this feeling all too well; I feared getting a doctorate because of Statistics and Quantitative Research. I had gotten a "C" or a barely "B" in almost every Statistics class I have taken since undergrad. To be honest, I did not only make a "C" in those courses, but I fought long and hard with tears to get the "C." I realized that getting my doctorate would mean that I would have to face two subjects that I hated. In fact, I recently finished both courses; I literally prepared my husband to take over the day-to-day operations of our home because I knew that I would be held captive in my office by these challenging courses. To my surprise, I had finally grasped the concepts; I finished both courses effortlessly with an "A." To think that I stunted my own growth over something that I already had the victory over.

I need you to grasp the idea that you cannot allow fear to drive the car when you want to be successful. Take your keys back from fear and take back control of your life. This concept is not solely about not being fearful about college, but I want you to apply this concept to every aspect of your life. Fear has a way of making obstacles look bigger than they actually are; so what if you face an obstacle and fail? Failing is a part of your story; at least you know what to expect the next time you face your opponent.

Let me ask you a question: are you actually afraid of the obstacle or are you really afraid of the work that it will take to beat the obstacle?

Big or small, all obstacles have a solution and sometimes many solutions. When you say, "I will" you are saying that you will do what it takes to face that obstacle and do WHATEVER it takes to overcome it. You will hear me say, "be specific" when it comes to your "I will" because generalities will hinder you from truly reaching your goals. This is what I mean by being specific with your "I wills."

Goal: Pass College Algebra

I Will:

Prior to taking the course, I will look at my math deficits and start reviewing concepts that I know are my weaknesses. I will connect with my College Algebra professor and let him or her know about my fear and struggles with math. I will seek out a small math group, I will sign up for Math Lab every Tuesday and will add Thursday if necessary.

Simple, I am not walking into any situation without a plan, especially a situation that I fear. I want to meet my goals, so to meet my goal, I have to look, re-alistically, at what it will take to meet it. I have not mastered this concept in every aspect of my life. But, I know that when I implement this way of thinking, I am able to do things beyond my wildest dreams.

Some months ago, my husband told me to resign from my position as an Educational Administrator. I was 31 years old when I got the position and I held it for three years before my husband made his, "you should resign" declaration. The position represented my accomplishments and my drive to work hard. It represented my ability to fight and work hard no matter what. If you said that I looked at an invisible Ms. Wilbur and said, "Aha, look at me," you wouldn't be wrong. I, Andrea Battle, 7th grade flunky got a position that many people had vied for. God blessed me immensely when I got this position. I was making over $90,000 a year, I had my own office, my own parking space. In my eyes, I had it all. Well, I had everything but peace. No matter how hard I worked or how much I pushed and prayed, the job left me with no peace. Then I realized that every job that I had leading up to that one left me in the same space; I went into the position, bright-eyed and bushy-tailed and always departed feeling disgusted and defeated. My husband had prayed about my situation and told me that it was time for me to walk away and use my drive and fire towards something that I believed in.

His words scared me, I thought to myself, *you want me to leave over $90,000 to create 'something' yeah right buddy.* Fear and I became best friends for a few months. I told my husband time and time again during those months that I was not leaving my job, but then one day, it hit me. In the middle of my one-hour commute to work one day, I heard God say, "Pack up your office." I was like, "huh?" "PACK UP YOUR OFFICE." I did not ask any more questions, I pulled into work, called my husband and said I am going to resign from my job. Astonished, he was like, "no way." I told him, "I am packing up my office now." Because I got to work way earlier than my employees, I was able to pack up my items and throw them in my SUV over the span of a couple of days.

I did not realize it at the time but packing up my office was symbolic. God knew that my fear needed an action. In order for me to move on, ' "move." Although my contract was until J had me move my stuff at the end of January and re-sign at the end of February. I have always depended on a job to sustain me; however, now that I am self-employed, I am learning that I don't need any partic-ular organization, but I need God, faith, and the fire that stays burning in the pit of my gut. I'm not saying that I won't ever work for someone, but I am saying that I will make all opportunities from now on to work for me as I build my empire.

Before I move away from fear, I want to debunk one other misconception about overcoming your fears. The suffering, challenge, pain, difficulty, or whatever will not ALWAYS last. The thing that you can always count on is that your obstacle has a time-line. Prepare yourself in advance for the sacrifice, pain, challenge or whatever comes with your obsta-cle, then face it head-on with faith. You've got this, do what it takes to receive the results that you want; you won't regret it.

I WILL: ADJUSTING

Adjusting is hard; if you didn't know this before, I am sure COVID-19 helped you to realize this fact. ADJUSTING. IS. HARD. If you are anything like me, you have experienced times where things were going perfectly fine and then the sky falls, and you are left to reinvent or start something new. I feel my best when I know what to expect; in fact, I have a habit of creating processes and routines. Getting married and having children gave me a crash course in the importance of being able to adjust. My children literally changed everything about me. My first daughter awakened at 2:00am in the morning, every morning; she started this preposterous habit in my womb. It was like she was having an all-out party in my stomach in the middle of the night—every night. As a person with a routine, this was problematic. "You are going to wake up at 2:00am EVERY MORNING?" I thought that this was just a phase in my pregnancy, but boy was I surprised when my darling infant that turned into an inquisitive toddler maintained the same habit. I had to adjust to her schedule and meet her needs.

Adjusting. Is. Hard.

No, it really is. I'm pretty sure I should have tattooed the word, "adjust" on my forearm 10 years ago when I married my husband. The first three years of marriage WAS SO FREAKING HARD! College Algebra is hard, Statistics is hard, losing weight is hard, but being married to another living breathing human being IS HARD. Plus, if you desire to maintain a healthy, loving relationship with the said human being, then you are going to have to know how to adjust.

I didn't know how to adjust at first, I honestly didn't. Instead of adjusting, I would complain and threaten divorce. I know you are judging me like, "Oh you are one of those." But let me explain. For one, divorce was an option for me at first because my parents divorced and two, we went through some crazy stuff.

After seven months of marriage, my husband lost his job. I am sure you have a certain understanding about me by now. I was devastated; here I am, a new-lywed with an unemployed husband. I didn't know a lot about being a wife, but I knew that I did not want to be the wife of a jobless man (don't the Bible say if a man don't work he don't eat?) Not to mention what he was probably feeling towards himself; I became his number one enemy. I was miserable. I was embarrassed and scared. I can remember laying upstairs in our townhouse when, in the middle of the night, a truck came and repossessed his vehicle. I can still hear the sounds of the loud engine and the sound the truck made as it reversed towards my husband's car. This was definitely not how I expected my life to go.

Somewhere and somehow, I felt in my spirit that I had to find a way to adjust. I. WILL. ADJUST. I stopped working against him and started working with him to get back on his feet. More than I wanted my marriage, I didn't want my marriage to fail. I didn't want to be like my parents. I wasn't them and their story was not my story. "I will adjust my thinking." I started considering how he felt about being unemployed, he did not lose his job on purpose or quit; I knew he loved being able to provide, and I knew above all else that he loved me and didn't want me to be unhappy. I felt the same. I held down the fort financially, we went to counseling, he got a job, we talked, and reset. Our adjusting took a lot of work, time, and dedication. If I had followed the culture of beating my man while he was down, I probably would not be married today. Oftentimes we only acknowledge our side of an issue, but what about the other person involved? In your adjusting, always consider what those around you are having to sacrifice; my husband had to face his new wife with a job loss. I could not imagine the mental anguish and self-loathing he experienced, but I am thankful that we were able to move past that difficult season!

Believe it or not, adjusting was a big part of our relationship even before we got married; I guess I didn't realize it because I wasn't the one doing the adjusting. I was a virgin when my husband and I got married. He wasn't a virgin and he was accustomed to having sex in his relationships. In the three years that we were together before marrying, he never asked for sex even once. He honored my wishes to abstain, and adjusted. He agreed to sharing our first intimate moments on our wedding day. Our abstinence wasn't a secret; everyone knew I was a virgin and that he wasn't; I guess they just waited to see how it would all play out.

I don't know all of the tips or tricks he used to wait for me, but I can remember a few times when he would tell me that he couldn't handle hugs that lingered or kisses that became passionate. In the first year, he would casually mention things that were difficult for him and I would quickly adjust. Besides that, he never made comments about how hard it was for him to wait or anything. I did not have an inkling of how hard it actually was for him to adjust until the day of our wedding when he and his groomsmen surrounded his Atlanta Falcons grooms cake and he cut the endzone that said, "Andrea" and his groomsmen put their arms up in a touchdown, "it's good" signal. Needless to say, he was relieved to make it to our wedding day. His willingness to adjust landed him a wife--a darn good one if I say so myself.

I have coached numerous couples who were struggling to adjust. Not to sound repetitive but adjusting IS hard. I tell them explicitly that they will struggle in the beginning, things will go well for a while, and then they will have to adjust again. Don't be fooled into believing that adjusting is a one-time thing. As long as you are in this world where all you can control is you, there will be reasons and seasons of adjustment. What you will have to do, though, is make up your mind that you will not allow the challenges that you are facing to change you without your consent.

Did you catch that message? When challenges arise, you will either adjust or the challenges will adjust you. Have you ever been on the highway and encountered an unforeseen detour? If you are anything like me, you probably have experienced a detour the same day that you were already running late to the most important interview of your career. To top it off, the detour is hard to follow and the traffic is horrific. How many times have you been tempted to just quit when you reached a detour of that magnitude? Maybe your detour is not literal but it is an instance where your job lays you off unexpectedly, perhaps the detour is a medical diagnosis, a tragic death in your family, or maybe your spouse had inappropriate contact with another individual leaving you feeling betrayed and uncertain about your future. How do you adjust when unforeseen detours occur?

You must have skills in your arsenal to handle abrupt changes. Like I have said previously, it is important that you make a plan and be specific. You can handle detours by saying, "I will adjust." While this statement is not an "abba cadabra" to your problems, it is a statement of preparation. By stating aloud, "I will adjust," you are robbing the issue of the ability to take complete control of your life; you are allowing yourself "think time" which could prevent you from an unhealthy response. Many of us have regretted our response to unforeseen issues. In this response, we become impulsive by quitting our job, divorcing our spouses, dissolving a friendship, etc. I want you to step away from impulsivity while you step into your adjusting season.

I don't want to live a life of regret because I handled an issue incorrectly. So many of us are quick to judge or react to other people's issues with a, "that couldn't be me" or with an, "I would have____, if that were me." Stop allowing others to project their ideals on your adjustment.

Maybe your best friend in the whole world refuses to believe that her sister's man actually kissed you; her sisters and their friends bully you on social media and make it seem like you are a homewrecker. The world joins in and bullies you too. How will you respond? What will you do to adjust? Will you allow the people that you trusted most to defame you and take you out? Or do you adjust by pushing forward, starting businesses, getting fit, finding new friends, joining the cast of the Masked Singer on Fox and using the infamy as a steppingstone to empowerment? That's what Jordyn Woods did; she adjusted! She did not let life's challenges to stop her. Instead, she grew!

It's totally up to you how you will respond and adjust to challenges; it is not for the world to decide how you respond. Life happens and mistakes happen. You have to adjust.

I was so excited August 2004 when I started at my university; Take that Ms. Wilbur! I worked my butt off and was an actual college student. To push the issue that I was a capable scholar, I decided that I would be a Biology (pre-dental) major. Little did I know that I absolutely sucked at Biology. I made low "Cs" and high "Ds." To top it off, I had never taken chemistry and had to withdraw. I could not believe it;

my GPA was suffering and I was totally bombing college. When I started to feel down and considered giving up, that fire in my stomach started to burn. I heard Ms. Wilbur's words replay over and over in my head. I reminded myself of my goals. I CAN. I WILL. I AM. I adjusted. I went to my college advisor and explored majors that I would actually enjoy and be good at. I realized that I would have to work hard to recover my GPA, but I did not care because I was college material and I was willing to adjust until I became what I believed and manifested it. Adjusting is hard, but it is absolutely necessary to reach your dreams.

Sometimes adjusting takes a conscious effort and sometimes it does not. You adjust all of the time, even when you don't realize it. Let's take cooking for instance; if you are cooking a meal and run out of an ingredient, you wouldn't throw the entire meal away. Instead, you will find a substitution. The substitution will either fill in the gap or it will take the meal a new direction. Don't let "missing ingredients" whatever "they" may be, cause you to completely give up. You must be willing to "fill" in the gaps with prayer, scripture, meditation—whatever! You were called to produce something, even in lack, you are expected to produce. Giving up is not an option; it's a choice and I want you to choose to move forward. Even if you have to move forward in another direction, don't ever stop moving.

It is important that you commit to adjusting; some of the most successful people learned how to adjust in the face of challenges and created amazing inventions and businesses because of their willingness to change direction or focus. Adjusting is an important skill; it takes willingness and acceptance; if we did not learn anything else from the COVID-19 season is that life as we know it can change at any moment, but it is not about the cause of the adjustment that matters, it is the response that makes all the difference. When issues far beyond your control arise, commit to making a move, tell yourself, "I Will Adjust!"

I AM

One of my 4-year-old twins was playing a racing game on my cell phone as I braided her hair. I was engaged in catching every tendril into a neat row of braids when I heard her chanting, "I can do it, I can do it, I can do it." When I looked at the cell phone screen, I did not see her opponent and assumed that she was in the lead. I stopped mid-braid and began rooting her on. I asked her how she will get over a certain obstacle, and she answered with confidence, "I will go around it." Somehow her game became my game and her win was my win. I watched her navigate the board with excitement; I looked at the top of the screen and to my dismay, her opponent was far ahead of her; she was losing—terribly. However, her four-year-old mind did not register a loss, but she was focused on navigating through the many obstacles that stood before her and the finish line. Even though she lost, she yelled, "I am a winner." Confused, I asked her, "Are you sure you are the winner?" She responded, "Look, I crossed the finish line."

You see, her indicator for success was not crossing the finish line before her opponent, but it was crossing the finish line. Even after her loss, she affirmed herself. She said, "I am a winner." She. Is. The. Winner. Because she sees herself as a winner, she is a winner.

If only we had this same confidence when we face life's challenges. We get so caught up in winning that we fail to see the power in losing. There is power in losing sometimes. Winning cannot be your only indicator for success! I want you to shift your thinking. You want to be successful, yet you are afraid of failure. What if I told you that you may have to fail to succeed? I want you to see failure differently. Failure is the beginning of your success story! Allow your failures to condition you for your successes. You don't have to win, to WIN.

I also need you to realize that you cannot connect who you are to what you've accomplished. I have made that mistake over and over again. I developed an overachiever mentality over the years; however, it became an unhealthy level of achieving. I identified as my achievements. You CANNOT identify yourself by what you achieve.

I have a sneaking suspicion that this may be the issue in Hollywood or with superstars in general. They become so entangled in their achievements that they wrap their entire identity into their persona and when they stop achieving or lose notoriety, many of them become overtaken by vices like overuse of alcohol, drug abuse, or unhealthy use of opiates.

You may not be in Hollywood or a celebrity, but you might be guilty of doing the same thing. Your identity is wrapped up in a GPA, a marriage, a church, a birth order, a clothing size, a group of friends, etc., and when that thing that you've become entangled with comes crashing down, you go crashing with it.

I want you to divorce that line of thinking. If you are worthy, awesome, and powerful because of the job, then what happens when the job is gone? What happens when the company goes bankrupt; do you lose value too?

The answer to that question is, "no!" You don't lose value because you brought value to the job; it did not bring value to you. You have to believe this dear heart. You are valuable just because...you are not valuable because your friends are cool or because you got accepted into an elite program. You are not worthy because you can do 50 push-ups; don't get me wrong, you ARE strong and can do probably 48 more push-ups than I can, but I still don't want you to wrap your identity around physical feats. You cannot identify as your physical attributes either; you are attractive. But so are many other people. You cannot place value in your looks because as we age, we gain weight, lose bone density, we lose hair, muscle mass, etc. I won't go on and on with this point but if you don't get anything else from this chapter, I want you to view yourself differently. I want you to start affirming yourself on a daily basis.

Ms. Wilbur did not realize it at the time, but she helped me with my very first affirmation, "I am college material." No seriously, "I AM COLLEGE MATERIAL." When those four words departed from my lips, it was as if my affirmation became a declaration—something in me clicked. You see, the "I can" helped me to evaluate what I was capable of doing to get into college, the "I will" caused me to be specific and activate my faith in God and myself, but the "I am" became a spring of living water. The words flowed from my mouth and flooded the atmosphere. My affirmation was so powerful that it did not allow for her to use the clear case that she had built against me—she was drowning in my proclamation.

I wish that I could tell you that this moment between Ms. Wilbur and I was an awe-inspiring made for TV moment. That she was this mentor archetype and that I was this underdog that she would take on this journey towards success. Instead, she almost gave me an antagonizing stare; I cannot remember if she sucked her teeth or not, but she definitely looked like she would leave me to write my own fate. I still to this day suspect that there were some racial motivators around the way she handled me, but that conversation is for another time.

But, she did leave me to write my own story; she did not have to provide me with one pen or one piece of paper because her words against me were more than enough. "I am college material." My own words became my adviser; they were with me when times were rough; when the classes became unbearable and tears threatened to fall from my eyes, my words wrapped around me like a grandmother's hug. When I was killing it and doing well, my words became my anthem; I was MIGHTY because I said I was mighty. There was absolutely nothing or anyone who could come between me and who I aspired to be.

I affirmed myself in every condition. Even now, 34-year-old Andrea exists from affirmation to affirmation: "I am beautiful," "I am strong," "I am a good wife," "I am an awesome mother." My "I ams" keep me on the yellow brick road towards my destiny. I say that success is at the tip of your tongue because your own words are one of the main determining factors to your destiny. As you may know from reading some of my story, I have not always been affirming and self-motivating. Some of you may not use affirmations now, but I encourage you to try affirmations out.

I AM COLLEGE MATERIAL; this affirmation was vital for my success and growth towards my goal. Without it, I am not sure that the "I can" or "I will" would have even mattered. Ms. Wilbur scathed at my "I can" pleas and she totally disbelieved my "I will" statements. But something changed when I said, "I am." Have you ever attempted to tell someone who you are to get them to leave you alone? I am so and so's sister or I am so and so's son. There are times that you have to say aloud who you are or who you belong to. I get this overwhelmingly amazing and warm feeling when I say, "I am the child of a King" or how God is a "Good Good Father." Allow your, "I am" mindset to rule. You won't regret it.

In the next few chapters, I want you to consider accepting a shift in perspective regarding who you are. From this point forward, I want you to receive every "you are" that I write as an, "I am." When I say you are powerful, I want you to receive it and say, "I am powerful!" I don't want you to follow that thought up with anything negative, but I want you to allow that thought to stand alone. You are powerful...that's it! Nothing else to follow.

"I am" is an affirmation and a call to fulfill your purpose. When you discover who you are and what you were created to do, then your affirmations make sense. You won't get stuck in a portal of self-doubt or bitterness when you are actually called to have a positive self-outlook. When I ask you who you are, I want you to answer with, "I am"

Who are you? "I am..." do you struggle to answer that question beyond simply stating your name?

When you say, "I am" you are giving yourself a title. Have you ever struggled to accept a title? I can totally agree with that feeling; when I started this journey, I changed my description on my Instagram account and I started a page on Facebook. In doing so, both platforms required that I put a description of who I am. It was so unnerving to allot an identity for myself. It was so challenging to say I am _____. With this new shift in my life, I had to bring some definition to who I am. I am still an educator, I will always be that, but my new identity is more aligned with who I aspire to be—an author, a coach, a motivator. Thus, I placed my new identity in the description box. While I did not have a formal life coach business, I would say with complete certainty that I have spent more time coaching people than I have educating them. This is coming from a 12-year educator.

It was challenging for me to settle in an identity because the world pushes you to be humble in some regards, but then at the same time inflate you in the wrong areas. A guilty pleasure of mine is to follow a page on Instagram called, "The Shade Room." This page is like the gossip blog of old, it is what TMZ used to be; however, it is in real time and "gossip" is at your fingertips. I could not explain it, at first, why this page was so entertaining to me, but I have finally put my finger on why it appeals to me so much. The Shade Room posts current happenings in the lives of stars; they post the good, the bad, and the ugly about the superstars of the world. They don't just report negativity, but they post celebrations also. I don't just read it for the posts that they make, but my favorite part is the comments. I love reading the comments because it gives me a gauge on how the world feels about a certain topic. I literally read hundreds of comments. I don't just read the comments that agree, but I love to follow a chain of comments where people disagree. When I see how different people perceive situations and issues in the world, I realize even more that you cannot wear the burden of acceptance. You cannot wear the burden of desiring acceptance because there will always be someone who will not accept you.

I want you to be who you are unapologetically because no matter what you do, there will be someone who disagrees with you. It doesn't matter how intelligent, well-versed, handsome, beautiful, muscular, or perfectly shaped an individual is on The Shade Room, someone in the comments will find an issue with that person. Even crazier, a star can be on top of the world on Monday and by Friday be the most hated in the world.

My Christian values are what I used to create my standards for living, any opinion, ideal, or construct outside of my religious values are moot. I suggest you do the same. Say "I am" and mean it!

I AM: JUST BECAUSE

Do you find yourself struggling to receive compliments? For a long time, I had an aversion to compliments. In fact, every now and again, I have to remind myself that it is okay for someone to say nice things about me. What's funny is that I was more receptive to the negative words spoken about me than the positive ones. I had become accustomed to being told that I had a bad attitude or that I was always angry, or that I had a resting "you know what" face. I accepted those words; the more that they were spoken over me, the more that I embodied them. I embraced them. I was them and they were me. Maybe I was angry; I had plenty to be upset about! I was angry even when I wasn't.

I'd be lying to you if I told you that Ms. Wilbur was the only educator that ever said something negative to me. The year that I failed the seventh grade, Ms. Clarke had me convinced that my final destination was prison. In fact, she said it in front of my peers. They would tease me and tell me that I would become some woman's _____ (insert bad word here) in prison.

I was disrespectful and bad, but did that make me a future inmate? If I had a weight for every Ill-willed word spoken over me, I would not be able to move. Grandma Billie was notorious for calling me names or spewing negativity at me. She would call me fat endlessly; even as an adult, she continued with her abusive conversation. After I reached puberty, I gained weight; when I visited her, the conversation always went the same way, "Hey, you're getting fatter every time I see you; you're gonna have diabetes." What a way to greet someone right? Or she would tell me how I was going to be screwed up like my mother was screwed up. She would tell me fake stories of my mother being strung out on drugs and her having to sober my mother up. Never mind the fact that in my 34 years of existence, I have never seen my mother touch any hard drug; in fact, she has the smallest tolerance for alcohol than anyone you've ever met. She can't handle more than a few sips before falling asleep. Plus, as her and my father's marriage neared

its end, she went from being a housewife to graduat-
ing nursing school. If you ask me, that is definitely
not a screw up (shrugs shoulders).

I still do not know what it served my Grandma
Billie to say such ridiculous things about my mother.
I don't know who she was trying to put down more —
me or her. Like Ms. Wilbur she didn't realize how
screwed up I actually was. "I am a screw-up;" that's
what I told myself every time I did something to get
in trouble. I can remember the day that the judge sen-
tenced me to six months probation. To give you con-
text, there was a girl in my neighborhood who con-
tinually tried to bully me; it was constant, excruciat-
ing, and aggressive. To this day, I still have no idea
why she disliked me. She lived near the park in our
neighborhood and she had apparently been watching
out her window as I took my little cousin to swing on
the swings. In the most scary and random manner she
popped up with a kitchen knife; she threatened to cut
me and my baby cousin. Just so you know, I had some
pretty horrible experiences growing up, but one thing
I can say is that I have always lived in great commu-
nities. Not rich, but always nice. I do not know what

uncouth hole she climbed out of, but she felt it necessary to pull a knife out and scare me and my cousin half to death. All we could do was run ALL. THE. WAY. HOME.

This girl taunted me; she called me the "b" word and threatened me literally every single day without fail. Until one day, I had enough. I could not take one more threat, I could not take one more vile insult. She was walking off the bus when she stopped at my seat and did her normal threat/b- word combo. I cannot explain what stood up in me that day, but I went from being a victim to a world-class boxer. I followed her off the bus, I am not sure what I said to her, I cannot remember who threw the first punch, but we fought and I won. I can remember sitting on her with her arms flushed to her side and hitting her in the face asking, "Who the B now, huh?" I got her for every bad word and for every threat she had expelled. I got her for making my life miserable, but especially for the fear she instilled in me and my baby cousin that day at the park. I would not have stopped if it were not for my mother's boyfriend spotting me as he drove through our neighborhood. He pulled up and demanded I get in the car. I got one more punch in as

I got up. I do not condone fighting in any shape, form, or fashion, but I had reached my breaking point. Needless to say, when I sat before the judge, I had earned my place in court.

Being called a screw-up, a future inmate, a female dog, and countless other names almost did a number on me; no wonder I struggled to receive compliments. Compliments contradicted what I had always heard and what I had always felt about myself. There came a time when I had to make peace with the words that had been belched out by my grandmother and countless others.

As a side note, be prepared to assist when your peers, siblings, children or whoever encounters a bully. There is something lasting about the words of a bully. I am not sure if there is research as to why the words of a bully are so lasting, but it is vital that a hard reset happens after a bully encounter. Don't be fooled into believing that only children have bullies. You can encounter a bully as an adult; in the workplace, we call them toxic individuals or individuals who create hostile work environments. It is absolutely necessary that you rid yourself of the harsh and damaging words or environment created by a bully or any negative force.

Affirmations are perfect to reset your mind from the traumas of a negative force. I use Scriptures and worship as a counter-attack to all negativity.

A few years ago, I received my first leadership position. I was so excited because I had got this position over some very qualified candidates. Unknown to me, I was about to work for the worst human I think I have ever met. I do not say this lightly; I don't know if this individual had a mental illness but this person was definitely the biggest bully I have ever met. When I first met my boss, I was excited because I thought they would be the perfect mentor. Boy, was I wrong! The individual sat in the office with all of the lights off with a lamp and the lowest watt bulb possible.

Walking into my boss's office was like entering a sunken place. This individual would have me complete all of these ridiculously long and intricate tasks and then when I finished them, they would tell me that they changed their mind or that they decided to go another direction; Sometimes they would not say

anything at all. I didn't realize it then, but it was in-
tentional. If this person kept me busy, then I would
not expect them to really do their job. I was so thrilled
about my financial raise and leadership opportunity
that I did not notice the abuse at first.

I would hear people say things about my boss; in
fact, several people warned me that my boss was hor-
rible, but I blew off their words as workplace gossip.
The first year was not that bad, it's like my boss spent
that year figuring out what made me tick and how I
could be broken down. Because my boss's job al-
lowed a lot of autonomy, my boss would go off the
grid for hours and sometimes days. When I would
ask simple questions or questions unrelated to my
boss's location, this individual would accuse me of
making up issues to find out where they were lo-
cated. First, my boss started off throwing subtle in-
sults like calling me a know-it-all or talkative. One
day, my boss straight up told me that my high energy
was annoying. The second year, I would get kicked
out of my boss's office and told that it was too early
for my up-beat energy.

We had individuals who were incessantly tardy or absent; tardiness and absences are highly problematic in a school building in general. It is unbearable in a school filled with challenging students. But, my boss would not allow me to say anything or would lie and say that the issue would be handled. Truth is, my boss didn't want to press the issue about tardiness or absences in fear that their off-the-grid behavior would be uncovered.

What I didn't know at the time was that our job was my boss's hiding place. It was with a group of difficult students who the world doesn't expect to learn. Instead of making a real difference, my boss perpetuated this "inability to learn" narrative as a way to hide.

The harder I worked, the more toxic my boss became. It took constant prayer to survive the years that I spent working in those toxic conditions. I went to therapy once I left to rid myself of the toxicity that tried to remain. Don't forget to reset after encountering a bully—I don't care who that bully is!

Thankfully, I had learned how to self-regulate my emotions and realized that I did not need to hear positive things consistently to know I was doing a good job. When I was younger, I can remember cringing when people told me, "good job" and especially when someone told me I was smart. In my head, I was a broken, 7th grade flunky. I wish I could help you visualize how broken I really was. If you could see it, like really see it, you would understand the power that affirmations have had—has in my life. Every, "I Am" helps me to see my world differently. Most of the time, I didn't have the words to speak over myself so I went to the Word of God for guidance on what to say to ME.

Let me reiterate that it is important that you allow yourself to receive compliments. Do not shy away from them, embrace them, swallow them whole and rub your belly as they satiate you. Use them how you see fit; I do not want you to rely solely on the positive affirmations but use them for your benefit. I want you to make a habit of saying positive things about yourself. Find Scriptures and authors who connect with who you desire to be. Most of the time people's words—whether positive or negative are not far off from your own thoughts. Find a way to rid yourself of the negative words and embrace the positive—the uplifting ones. There is a thin line between constructive criticism and negativity. Don't allow anyone else's words, whether positive or negative, to penetrate any deeper than your own words.

The idea of being a "screw-up" had been engrained so deep within me that even when I did positive and great things, I would diminish them. Now, there is nothing that anyone can say negatively that impacts me on any level. I recognize what deserves acknowledgement and what should be ignored. I have finally realized that I do not have to make excuses for who I am, what I do, or how I feel. I now know that I don't have to prove myself to anyone.

Whether it is a mean grandmother, an unsupportive school counselor, the neighborhood bully, or a horrible boss, no one has the right to demean or degrade you. When people try to place you in any other category except the one that you belong, you stand flat-footed and tell them, " I Am; Just because!"

I AM: TIMING

Timing is everything! Have you ever considered the role that timing plays in your life, opportunities, choices, etc.? After I stood my ground with Ms. Wilbur, and declared that I was no longer who my records characterized me as, more than a physical change in classes occurred. It was like a time shift or what I have always considered my "season" changed. I could not articulate it at the time, but it was this ethereal moment where I could literally feel a shift in my life. It was palpable; it was heavy. It wasn't a burden, but it was a spiritual confirmation—an awakening. My declaration and my affirmation became a "timing" machine. I was carried away from this angry, sexually abused kid, whose parents had divorced into someone different.

Even I didn't recognize me.

You see after my fight on the street corner with the knife toting bully, my mother sent me to Virginia to live with my aunt so that I could be close to my daddy. She was over my shenanigans and the probation was the last straw. I was a daddy's girl and she knew it. She felt I needed time to be near him; I didn't know it then, but she really just wanted me to see that he was still in a very selfish phase and the person that I was yearning to be near was a person who wanted to be a bachelor. Because I lived with my mother primarily and she had to be the disciplinarian and the provider, I had grown resentful towards her. I resented that she and my dad didn't work. I resented that we had to live so far away. I resented the 16-hour shifts that she had to work to keep us living in a good neighborhood.

When I moved in with my aunt Patty, my daddy and my relationship was everything but magical. I stayed in Virginia for one school semester; I sat around waiting for something to spark. I wanted my dad to be instantly like a sitcom dad. I had imagined this magical connection and had yearned for his attention. After reality set in, I begged my mom to return home. I was home by my second semester of ninth grade. I was so hurt about my time in Virginia that I really became hopeless. My return did not change anything; my mother was still working 16-

hour shifts. My sister, Casey, was completing her first year of college in Georgia. I missed her so much. I was lonely and lost; I continued to misbehave and had low grades.

Over the summer, my sister and her best friend Lauren (who I also refer to as my sister) moved into an apartment near their college campus. Even in this moment, I get chills to think about how God is always in the details. God must have whispered in their ears; Casey and Lauren noticed that there was a bus stop a few feet from their apartment and wondered if I could move to Georgia with them.

Two college students—one sophomore and one junior wanted a 15-year-old troubled teen to come and live with them. Even more abnormal was that my mother agreed. You wouldn't understand it unless you have an older sister, but the maternal connection between an older sister and her younger sibling(s) is powerful. It's truly like having two mothers.

My mother was okay with allowing her youngest child to go live with college students. Although she was (and still is) in a relationship with a man 11 years younger than her, I now suspect that she, too, desired to live the bachelorette life. To be honest, I feel like she deserved it; she deserved the break! My sisters provided her refuge and relieved her of the guilt of her workaholism.

When sharing my story recently, someone asked if I had perceived my mother dropping me off as abandonment. I cannot answer that question. I know that she loves me, but I also know that she has had her own traumas that she had to learn to get past. Perhaps her leaving me felt like abandonment in the back of my mind, but even more was the relief I felt when I got to Georgia. Have you ever had an itch that you could not reach, or have you ever known you needed to be somewhere, but it wasn't until you got there that you realized that it is where you were supposed to be? I felt this, when I got to Georgia. I felt like I had finally reached the itch, and I was scratching it with all of my might. It was like things had finally aligned perfectly; for the first time in my entire life, I felt like I was in the right place.

When you are in the right place, it does not matter how many Ms. Wilburs you encounter because even their existence is important for you to move forward.

I am not one of those people who say that God put me through horrific traumas for whatever reason people give. Neither do I believe that it was God's will for my life to be sexually and physically abused, for my parents to divorce, or to be a smelly middle schooler, but I do believe He allowed good to ultimately come out of it.

Within the first few months of coming to Georgia, I connected with some individuals who I still revere as my extended family to this day. They were far more than my church family, they were like blood. Being 15 years old, in another state, my pastor, first lady, his sister the evangelist, her husband the youth pastor, and one of our deacons became like parents to me. My deacon-dad drove me back and forth to summer school when I was re-taking geometry. My extended family were there when I graduated from high school and college, my pastor-daddy performed my wedding. My first lady-mom coached me through my first year of marriage. My Mama V, the evangelist, let me and my oldest stay over when she was only a few days old because my husband had just started a program and my daughter was premature. I could go on and on about how much they were there for me

103

and loved me, my hubby, and children. God, in all His wisdom, knew just what I needed to grow beyond my torrential past.

Timing is everything; somehow, I went from an overwhelming lack to exceeding abundance. Abundantly loved and abundantly cared for. Thank God for His perfect timing!

I AM: MY OWN ADVOCATE

"It seems like you have depended on others to advocate for you, but is it possible that they believe that you are capable of advocating for yourself?" **- My Therapist**

Whenever a therapist says, "but is it possible that..." be ready to give up any ideals, blames, or constructs that you have developed about any given situation.

When my granny passed away in 2014; she was over 600 miles away in Flint Michigan. She died unexpectedly from a heart attack early that morning. My big cousin, Michael, called to deliver the horrible news. Being far away from a death of that magnitude is pretty much the worst thing on earth. As my father's only biological child, I had to weather the storm of her unexpected death ALL BY MYSELF. It's not that my husband did not know or love her, but he did not have the hugs, the late-night conversations, the delicious meals, or the amazing memories. My granny was one of my favorite people in the world.

She had never hit me, raised her voice at me, or anything. We would stay on the phone for hours talking about any and everything. I can still, at this moment, hear her voice and her laugh.

I know that I said that my granny was one of my favorite people, but for my dad, she was his world—literally. They spoke EVERY. SINGLE. DAY. without fail. He was her youngest, "unexpected," child. She would tell me, in jest, how she was allergic to latex and how if birth control was available like it is now, my father would not be here. Wait, neither would I—right?

My daddy has recounted, numerous times, the last night that they spoke. From his description, she had sounded winded, but he had blamed it on her allergies. Some of us in our family believe that it was her older sister's death just months before that literally broke her heart. Her and my dad's last conversation wasn't long, but the conversation ended with, "I love you." I am thankful that it ended that way.

After half-way swallowing the shock of her passing, I sat quietly in my living room; I knew that I had to call my daddy, but what would I say? Michael told me that my daddy knew that she had passed, but what do you say to someone who loved their mother as deeply as my father did?

The phone rang…he answered. He sounded ok, why did he sound okay? He wasn't okay; I wasn't okay. We did not speak long; the conversation wasn't anything like I had expected. I asked him about his plans to drive from Virginia to Michigan, and he said that he would definitely drive. I told him that I would fly; he agreed that I should fly. His calmness caused my heart to race. Why is he so calm? "I will fly to you daddy; I want to ride in the car with you daddy." He agreed; he was heading to work. "To work daddy?" I questioned. "Yes, I am going to work," he responds.

There is something powerful about collective grief; everyone piling up at the deceased person's home with food, drinks, laughs, and cries. Being hundreds of miles away from family, no one understood my mourning. My husband knew my granny and I believe he loved her, but he did not have the 28 years of experience and deep-rooted love that I had for her. He sat by my side and consoled me; but in that moment, I felt like I needed more. I had agreed, previously, to do his niece's hair in braids that would take a long time. Before this change of events, it was no big deal for me to do her hair. In fact, I had welcomed the visit to see her, my other niece, and nephew.

But the moment that I received the call, everything changed for me; I did not want to see anyone, I did not want to do her hair, I wanted to drop everything and run to Virginia and be by my father's side. I wanted to share a cry with someone who understood what an amazing woman we had lost. I wanted to be with my cousins. I was devastated. At that moment, I didn't care about anyone or anything; I was worried, deeply, about my father.

The time drew closer for us to go to my brother in law's home so I could do my niece's hair. I was miserable. I didn't want to go; why couldn't my husband see that I didn't want to go? Why didn't he recognize the loss that I had just experienced and tell me, "No, take care of yourself"? I had held some resentment towards him for not speaking up for me. I was so disappointed in him. Looking back, I was being very unreasonable.

"Maybe he didn't tell you to take care of yourself because he assumed that doing your niece's hair would take your mind off of the pain. Did you tell him differently? I notice that this is a recurring theme...it seems like you have depended on others to advocate for you, but is it possible that they believe that you are capable of advocating for yourself?" You guessed it—**My Therapist.**

Of course, she was completely correct in her assessment. Even more than his lack of knowledge regarding my needs; I had totally assumed at that moment that he was emotionally available to attend to my issues. We cannot discount the needs of those that we depend on; we cannot always assume that others are available to meet our needs. There will be more times than not that you will need to be your own advocate. Repeat after me:

I am my own advocate.

You are your own advocate. But first, you have to define what that looks like to you. For some of us, being our own advocate is simply speaking up for ourselves. My granny had passed away and I was in an unstable emotional space. I was in shock, I was anxious, and extremely sad. I should have told my niece that I could not do her hair. That one little moment of advocating for myself would have prevented me from holding a small but unnecessary resentment for my husband.

Advocating for yourself may be your unwillingness to accept "no" or those dreadful, "you are not(s)." It is up to you to fight for what you perceive as being right for you! I have heard stories of medical doctors prescribing interventions and medicines that an individual does not agree with. Unnecessary medicines can affect your overall health. It does not matter what credentials a doctor or anyone else has; if it is not right for you, then it is not RIGHT.

It is okay to stand up for yourself and tell someone how you desire to be treated—whether it be a medical treatment or personal treatment. Contrary to popular belief, you are part owner of your body, mind, and soul. The co-owner is our Heavenly Father. However, even God gives us a will and the ability to choose. He allows us to advocate for ourselves in prayer.

You are your own advocate at work, at school, at home, in the bank, at the mall, at the doctor's office, with your mom, with your children, with your siblings, WHEREVER YOU ARE! Your inner advocate should be there!

Over the last couple of years, I have coached several couples through challenging in-law situations. For some reason, parents will encourage you to, "read your Bible" and be the constant reminder to, "follow what the Word of God says." But when it is their turn, they totally disregard the part of the Bible that talks about their son or daughter cleaving to their spouse. When you marry, you instantly become the advocate for your family unit. That family unit no longer includes your parents or your siblings. It is your duty to support your spouse and children. I am not telling you to disrespect or dishonor your parents, but I am saying that no one else has a say so in your home and it is your duty to advocate for your spouse. We have all heard stories of the overbearing in-laws. They may seem powerful, but they only have the power that you give them.

No one has more power than the power that you give them. If you have a toxic friend and you continue to allow him or her to speak down on your dreams and aspirations, then you are the problem, not them. When you allow or welcome others to devalue you, you have to recognize your role. You have to advocate for yourself in ALL situations.

Please know that I am not speaking from a place of perfection; I am learning, every day, how to advocate for myself. Here are a few tips to self-advocacy:

- Be more expressive!

- Express when you have a need.

- Don't be afraid to tell someone to stop doing something that you do not like.

- Be willing to tell your doctor or any professional "no" when it is necessary. Their professional knowledge does not supersede what you know in your spirit about you!

- Create boundaries so that you know you are less afraid of using your voice to speak up.

THE GAS-UP

There is a saying that we use in the urban vernacular called, "gas up;" it has absolutely nothing to do with "gas" but everything to do with providing fuel to someone else, figuratively. To gas someone up is to build them up through kind words, compliments, giving them positive praise, or just inflating their ego. I have decided to devote one of the last chapters of my book to gassing you up! I know that most of this text has included stories and anecdotes of my life, but it is my desire that you see my life as a testimony. You have access to whatever life you want, but you have to see and speak what you want out of life. I am not a theologian, nor biblical scholar, but I want you to know that this "gas up" is a blessing that I am speaking over you. I don't know where you are right now as you read this text, but I want you to sit up straight and receive every single word that I declare.

YOU CAN; say it for me one last time, say, "I CAN!"

YOU CAN, my friend. You are SO powerful; you look at challenges, disappointments, and impossibilities and you see OPPORTUNITIES. Your, "I can," is a declaration to the world and the atmosphere that you may not be able to change your situation but you recognize that there are things that you "Can" do. You are willing to do the work that it takes to go to the next level. You have identified your struggles and are working around them. You see failures as opportunities to try again. You are not allowing any negativity from your past to rob you of a positive future. You have a spirit of discernment; you recognize who and what is good for you and you annihilate anything that is bad for you. You can hear from God; you are sensitive to His will for your life.

You don't see walls as barriers, but as opportunities to reach higher heights.

When you say, "I Can," you are not saying to others that they cannot, but you are finally recognizing your worth and value.

Friend, I want to remind you that in addition to the "I Can" statement that you have embodied, you also "will;" say it out loud and with girt declare it, "I will." YOU WILL take the steps necessary to reach your goals. You will not procrastinate, but you will assassinate anything that is hindering you. You are a BEAST and you are demolishing all laziness, low self-esteem, self-doubt, and self-loathing. You have an aversion to inactivity; in fact, you are going to push yourself harder than ever before.

Say it and mean it. With a stern voice state, "I WILL push myself." You will not settle; you will use every single second in the 24 hours given to you in a meaningful way. You will press when you feel like stopping. You will stop when you are over-functioning and you will listen to your body when it is time to rest. You will speak up for yourself when loud voices surround you and try to drown you out. You will humble yourself, when necessary, and not say a word because your life and your work is speaking loud and clear!

You will make the changes necessary to go to the next level; you will lose weight, you will forgive, you will dream again, you will stop procrastinating, you will overcome fears and doubts. You will adjust when everything is falling apart around you. You will seek counseling to deal with the hidden disappointments, the unresolved issues, the pain that keeps you awake, or the mental anguish that causes you to sleep your life away. You will take the rain from your rainy days and grow. You will accept that you have the power because you do; you have the power to reach your dreams and to make big moves.

You will "Faith it till you make it!" You have a BIG FAITH in a BIG GOD who is capable of supplying all of your needs. You will believe in yourself again. In the face of the fight of your life, you will have faith until you get to the place you want to be. You will have the faith that is necessary to walk on water. Taking that first step doesn't mean you won't sink, but it means that you are willing to make a move that is worth sinking for. Take that step, sink, one day you'll float!

You will believe again; you have looked up to people and they have let you down. You have used their let-down as an excuse for you to stay down, but

NOT ANYMORE. Today is the day that YOU WILL get up. Say it! Say, "I WILL get up." Yes, you will! You will get up out of that sunken place.

Lastly, I want to remind you who you are; place your hand in the middle of your chest and declare, "I Am."

You are...YOU ARE ROYALTY. I don't mean that in a cliché fairytale way, but I mean it. You are the Child of a King. The only reason why you don't feel royal is because you feel like you have been inundated with so many trials. But even Shakespeare said, "Heavy is the head that wears the crown;" you are misreading your heaviness as lowliness. You are not in a low place, but you are sitting high. Accept who you are and who God created you to be. As a royal, you have a purpose to fulfill, you have work to do to keep the kingdom moving.

You are positive. From this day forward, you are only speaking positivity over your own life. Say this, say, "I am healthy." You are HEALTHY—physically, mentally, and emotionally. You are healthy; you make healthy decisions, you surround yourself with healthy people, and you recognize when things are not good for your mental or physical health.

You are! You are worthy; you are so worthy! I don't care if someone in your past told you otherwise, I am telling you right now--you are worthy. I know that you are living in a world that refuses to see your worth but be encouraged. You are worthy and immensely valuable. Things may not look encouraging in the news, on social media, in your family—wherever! But you are the positivity that the world needs today. You bring value to this world with every positive step that you take. Every encouragement that you post on social media, every time that you speak into the lives of the youth, colleagues, family members, anyone, realize that you are putting your value on display.

You Can! You Will! You Are!

I CAN! I WILL! I AM!: THE WRAP-UP

I would love to tell you that I have reached a place of perfection after everything that I have gone through, but I am continually finding faith, facing fears, and speaking success. The process of, "I Can, I Will, I Am" is ongoing and a daily practice. None of us considers the residual issues that remain after traumas occur; as you may imagine, every now and again, I find myself uncovering hidden issues. But I have hope that one day I will be whole and have complete victory over the challenges I have faced.

Writing this book has brought such healing and hope into my life. During the course of writing this book, I have gone to biweekly therapy, I have spent intimate time with both of my parents, my family, I have reached out and loved on my grandma Billie, I have reminisced, I have challenged thinking, I have torn down walls. I did not share every high nor did I share every low, but I hope what I gave you was enough to encourage you to move forward in your walk. I hope that you completely embody the, "I Can, I Will, I Am" mindset!

One of my good friends, who I went to high school with, looked up and found Ms. Wilbur. Although I was tempted, I did not reach out to her. I have considered sending her this book and letting her know that I changed her name to Ms. Wilbur. I can only hope that she refrained from telling another child, "YOU. ARE. NOT." It's my prayer that her time with me was just a fluke—that she was having a bad day. Bless you, Ms. Wilbur; thank you for thrusting me forward.

It is a sentimental feeling to reach the end of my, "I will write a book," chapter. I had a goal to write and self-publish a book before starting my dissertation and I have met that goal. I am immensely thankful to God for His grace and mercy that has kept me through this unique and difficult ride. While I know that many others have had far harder lives than I, I am still thankful for all that God has kept me through.

As I type these last few words, I want to express my thankfulness for this journey and the time that you took to read my story. I would like to end with a prayer and share some Scriptures that have impacted my life.

Dear Lord,

First, we come before You with thanksgiving; Father, we thank You for Your grace and mercy, we thank You for divine favor and for ordering our footsteps. Even in the midst of challenges, uncertainties, and unexpected storms, You have been faithful. God, You deserve the glory for un-covering issues and covering us all with Your mighty hand. We thank You as we learn to say "I Can" when we don't know what to do. We honor You for offering us the faith to say, "I Will" although sometimes we don't want to, and lastly God, we praise You for the "I Am." You have taught us how to speak over our own lives, and the im-portance of speaking blessings over those around us. Lord, Your Word showed us the power of the "I Am" all the way back when You spoke to Moses, we know that You have given us the power as Your sons and daughters; we have access to faith, power over fear, and the ability to speak suc-cess. Bless us as we all take this challenging journey called life; we will always give You the glory and honor for all things. Thank You for, "I Can, I Will, I Am: Finding Faith, Facing Fears, and Speaking Success." You are a mighty and awesome Father! In Jesus' precious name, Amen.

Psalm 139:14 NIV

Finally, brothers and sisters, whatever is true, whatever is noble, whatever is right, whatever is pure, whatever is lovely, whatever is admirable—if anything is excellent or praiseworthy—think about such things.

Proverbs 3:5 NIV

Trust in the Lord with all your heart and lean not on your own understanding;

Romans 8:31 NIV

What, then, shall we say *in* response to these things? If God is for us, who can be against us?

Philippians 1:6 NIV

Being confident of this, that he who began a good work *in* you will carry it on to completion until the day of Christ Jesus.

Philippians 4:6-8 NIV

Do not be anxious about anything, but in every situation, by prayer and petition, with thanksgiving, present your requests to God. And the peace of God, which transcends all understanding, will guard your hearts and your minds in Christ Jesus. Finally, brothers and sisters, whatever is true, whatever is noble, whatever is right, whatever is pure, whatever is lovely, whatever is admirable—if anything is excellent or praiseworthy—think about such things.

Jeremiah 29:11 NIV

For I know the plans I have for you," declares the Lord, "plans to prosper you and not to harm you, plans to give you hope and a future.

Romans 8:28 NIV

And we know that *in* all things God works for the good of those who love him, who have been called according to his purpose.

Psalm 147:3 NIV

He heals the brokenhearted and binds up their wounds.

NOW BEGIN YOUR NEXT CHAPTER

I Can | I Will | I Am

May your next chapter be your BEST CHAPTER

-AB

Made in the USA
Columbia, SC
22 February 2023

12826252R00072